T0105188

the LAUGH GIRAFFE'S

BEST AND FUNNIEST
ANIMAL JOKES

the LAUGH GIRAFFE'S
BEST AND FUNNIEST
ANIMAL JOKES

350 Highly Hilarious Jokes!

Sky Pony Press
New York

Sky Pony Press books may be purchased in bulk at special discounts for sales promotion, corporate gifts, fund-raising, or educational purposes. Special editions can also be created to specifications. For details, contact the Special Sales Department, Sky Pony Press, 307 West 36th Street, 11th Floor, New York, NY 10018 or info@skyhorsepublishing.com.

Sky Pony® is a registered trademark of Skyhorse Publishing, Inc.®, a Delaware corporation.

Visit our website at www.skyponypress.com.

10 9 8 7 6 5 4 3 2 1

Manufactured in China, 2020
This product conforms to CPSIA 2008

Library of Congress Cataloging-in-Publication Data is available on file.

ISBN: 978-1-5107-5865-0
EISBN: 978-1-5107-5866-7

Cover design by Daniel Brount
Illustrations by Alex Paterson

Printed in China

the LAUGH GIRAFFE'S
BEST AND FUNNIEST
ANIMAL JOKES

Why does a giraffe have such

a long neck?

Because his feet stink!

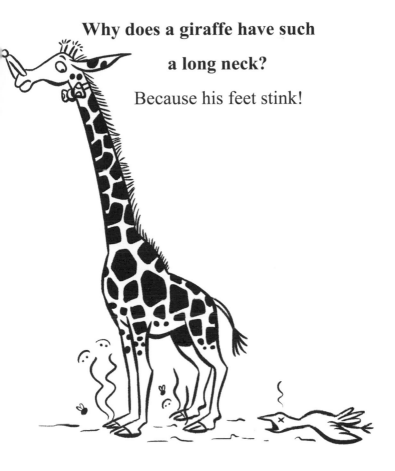

☆

Why does it take a giraffe a long

time to apologize?

Because it takes a long time for

them to swallow their pride!

☆

What's green and hangs from trees?

Giraffe snot!

☆

What time is it when an elephant sits on a fence?

Time to get the fence fixed!

☆

What do you call an alligator wearing a vest?

An in-vest-igator!

☆

What do you call a lazy baby kangaroo?

A pouch potato!

☆

What was the pig doing in the kitchen?

Bacon!

☆

Why can't you have a good conversation with a goat?

It always butts in!

☆

How do dog catchers get paid?

By the pound!

☆

What do you get if you cross a snake with a builder?

A boa constructor!

☆

What's striped and bouncy?

A tiger on a pogo stick!

What do cats like to drink?

Purr-fied water!

☆

What kind of animals have the best memories?

Turtles. They have turtle recall!

☆

What do you get when you cross a sheep with a porcupine?

An animal that can knit sweaters!

☆

What animal should you never play cards with?

Cheetahs!

☆

What has fifty legs but can't walk?

Half a centipede!

☆

How do snails fight?

They slug it out!

☆

What do cows get in the mail?

Cattle-logs!

☆

Why do seagulls fly over the sea?

Because if they flew over the bay they'd be bay-gulls!

☆

THE LAUGH GIRAFFE'S
BEST AND FUNNIEST ANIMAL JOKES

What kind of key opens a banana?

A monkey!

☆

Why don't oysters donate to charity?

Because they are shellfish!

☆

How do you know that a mouse needs oiling?

It squeaks!

☆

What's a cat's favorite color?

Purrr-ple!

☆

Why did the watchdog run in circles?

Because he was winding himself!

☆

What do you call a monkey who eats potato chips?

A chip-monk!

☆

Why do cows never have any money?

Because farmers milk them dry!

☆

THE LAUGH GIRAFFE'S
BEST AND FUNNIEST ANIMAL JOKES

What do you call a fish without an eye?

Fsh!

☆

What do you call a fish with no eyes?

Fishually impaired!

☆

How do you make a goldfish old?

Takc away the G!

☆

What do you call a sleeping bull?

A bull-dozer!

☆

Why did the Dalmatian go to the eye doctor?

He kept seeing spots!

☆

How do you make a baby snake cry?

Take away its rattle!

☆

How are a dog and a marine biologist different?

One wags a tail, the other tags a whale!

☆

Why do owls get invited to parties?

Because they're a hoot!

☆

Why do polar bears and penguins not get along?

Because they are polar opposites!

Why was the mouse afraid to go in the lake?

Catfish!

☆

What's orange and sounds like a parrot?

A carrot!

☆

What do you get if you cross a hyena and a cow?

The laughing stock of the community!

☆

What did the buffalo say when his boy went to school?

Bi-son!

☆

Why do dogs run in circles?

It's too hard to run in squares!

☆

Doctor, doctor, I think I'm a goat.

How long have you felt like this?

Since I was a kid!

☆

Why aren't cows good dancers?

They have two left feet!

☆

Why do monkeys like bananas?

Because they have a peel!

☆

Why are giraffes good students?

Because they're head and shoulders

above the rest of the class!

☆

THE LAUGH GIRAFFE'S
BEST AND FUNNIEST ANIMAL JOKES

What do you call an angry monkey?

Furious George!

☆

What do lions serve at parties?

Chimps and dip!

☆

What do you call shaving a crazy sheep?

Shear madness!

☆

What is the difference between an bull and a car?

A bull has two horns!

☆

What do you call an alligatore with a GPS?

A navi-gator!

☆

What do you get from a shark?

You get as far away as possible!

☆

Why is a swordfish's nose only 11 inches long?

Because if it were 12 inches it would be a foot!

☆

What do dogs eat for breakfast?

Pooched eggs!

☆

Why do centipedes have 100 legs?

So they can walk!

☆

Why was the crow on the telephone wire?

To make a long distance caw!

☆

What do you get if you cross a chicken and a centipede?

Enough drumsticks for the whole family!

☆

Where do sheep get their haircuts?

At the baa-baa shop!

☆

Why should you never share a bed with pigs?

They hog the covers!

☆

Did you hear about the cannibal lion?

He swallowed his pride!

☆

Why are elephants gray?

So you can tell them apart from flamingos!

THE LAUGH GIRAFFE'S
BEST AND FUNNIEST ANIMAL JOKES

What did the beaver say to the tree?

It's been nice gnawing you!

☆

Why did the dog sit in the shade?

Because he heard people eat hot dogs!

☆

What did the dog say to the bun?

Are you pure bread?

☆

What is the lion's favorite cookie?

Chocolate chimp!

☆

What did the grape say when the elephant stepped on it?

Nothing. It just gave a little wine!

☆

What do you call a baby monkey?

A chimp off the old block!

☆

What do you get when you have four ducks in a box?

A box of quackers!

☆

Why do they call it a litter of puppies?

Because they mess up the whole house!

☆

Where do gorillas get their gossip?

On the ape vine!

☆

Where do orcas play music?

In orca-stras!

☆

How do you catch a runaway dog?

Hide behind a tree and make a noise
like a bone!

☆

What's worse than raining cats and dogs?
Hailing taxis!

☆

Did you hear about the hen that only laid eggs in three seasons?
She was no spring chicken!

☆

How do pigs send secret messages?
With invisible oink!

☆

What kind of ant is as big as an elephant?
A gi-ant!

☆

**Why should you not write a book
    on penguins?**
Because writing a book on paper is
    much easier!

☆

**What did the shark say after
    eating the clown fish?**
This tastes funny!

☆

Why was the lobster embarrassed?
Because the sea-weed!

☆

Why are octopuses good at war?
They are well armed!

☆

Why do lions eat raw meat?

Because they can't cook!

☆

Why did the boy take his dog to the watchmaker?

It had ticks!

☆

Why do dogs need a license but cats don't?

Cats can't drive!

☆

How do you get an escaped monkey back in his cage?

With a bargaining chimp!

☆

What came after the dinosaur?

Its tail!

☆

Why wasn't the octopus in the zoo?

He joined the Arm-y!

☆

What do you get when two giraffes run into each other?

A gir-affic jam!

☆

What time is it when an elephant sits on your bed?

Time to get a new bed!

☆

What do you call a frozen dog?

A pupsicle!

☆

Where does an elephant sit?

Anywhere he wants to!

☆

Why don't chickens like people?

Because they beat eggs!

☆

What's gray and stands in the rain but doesn't get wet?

An elephant with an umbrella!

☆

What did the squirrel say to his girlfriend?

I'm nuts about you!

☆

Why was the dog chasing his tail?

He was trying to make ends meet!

☆

What kind of dog does Dracula have?

A bloodhound!

☆

When can't you reach the zoo on the phone?

When all the lions are busy!

☆

Why are cats good at video games?

Because they have nine lives!

☆

What animals do you need to make a rectangle?

Four lions!

☆

What kind of floors do you find in zoos?

Rep-tiles!

☆

What did the Dalmatian dog say after he ate his dinner?

That hit the spots!

☆

Why do waiters like gorillas better than flies?

Nobody ever complained about a gorilla in their soup!

☆

Why did the moth eat a hole in the rug?

He wanted to see the floor show!

☆

Where do fish keep their money?

In a river bank!

☆

Why do cats always get their way?

Because they are very purr-suasive!

☆

How did the cat do on the test?

Purr-fect!

☆

**What do you get when you cross a
pig and a giraffe?**

Bacon and legs!

THE LAUGH GIRAFFE'S
BEST AND FUNNIEST ANIMAL JOKES

If a rooster layed an egg on a sloped roof, would it fall to the left or right?

Neither. Roosters don't let eggs!

Why do hummingbirds hum?

Because they don't know the words!

How much does a lion tamer have to know?

More than the lion!

What do you call an angry pig?

Disgruntled!

What happened when the owl lost his voice?

He didn't give a hoot!

☆

What did the banana say to the monkey?

Nothing. Bananas can't talk!

☆

What do dogs do after they finish obedience school?

They get their masters!

☆

What else do dogs get when they finish obedience school?

Their pet-degrees!

☆

Where do sharks go for vacation?

Fin-land!

☆

When is the best time to buy a bird?

When they are going "cheep!"

☆

What did the doctor say to the sick bat?

Hang in there!

☆

What do you call an animal you keep in your car?

A car-pet!

☆

Why did the chicken cross the playground?

To get to the other slide!

☆

What kind of dinosaur has a big vocabulary?

A thesaurus!

☆

Can you name 10 dinosaurs in five seconds?

3 velociraptors and 7 brontosauruses!

☆

Why do birds fly south in the winter?

It's too far to walk!

☆

What game did the cat play with the mouse?

Catch!

☆

Why can't you fool a snake?

It doesn't have any legs to pull!

☆

What do you get if you cross a parrot and a woodpecker?

A bird that talks in Morse code!

How do cats maintain the peace?

With claw enforcement!

☆

What did the cat say to the bad joke?

You've got to be kitten me!

☆

Where do cats go when they lose their tails?

To a re-tail store!

☆

What's another name for a wasp?

A wanna-bee!

☆

What do you call a show full of lions?

The mane event!

☆

Why was the duck arrested?

It was accused of fowl play!

☆

Why do cows lie down together when it is cold?

To keep each udder warm!

☆

How do cats end a fight?

They hiss and make up!

☆

Why do ducks make good detectives?

They always quack the case!

☆

How do chickens leave a chicken coop?

They use the eggs-it!

☆

Where do baby cows go for lunch?

The calf-eteria!

☆

Where do rabbits eat pancakes?

At IHOP!

☆

Why did the giant ape climb up the side of the skyscraper?

Because the elevator was broken!

☆

What is the best month to see gorillas?

Ape-ril!

☆

What do you call a pile of kittens?

A meow-tain!

☆

Why did the farmer name his pig Ink?

Because he was always running out of the pen!

☆

How do you know that carrots are good for your eyes?
Did you ever see a rabbit with glasses?

☆

How do you know dead canaries are expensive?
Because they don't go cheep!

☆

Why can't dinosaurs laugh?
Because they're dead!

☆

What do you call a rabbit with fleas?
Bugs, bunny!

☆

What is the best way to get in touch with a fish?

Drop it a line!

☆

What do you call a lion running the copying machine?

A copycat!

☆

Why did the crab get arrested?

Because he was always pinching things!

☆

How do you keep a dog from barking in your front yard?

Put him in your back yard!

☆

What kind of horse is good at swimming?

A seahorse!

☆

What kind of monkey is good at sports?

A chimpion!

☆

Why shouldn't dogs race to the door when the doorbell rings?

It's hardly ever for them!

☆

What do you call farm animals with a sense of humor?

Laughing stock!

☆

On which day do lions eat people?

On chewsday!

☆

What happens when you try to cross a lion and a goat?

You need a new goat!

☆

What do you call a confused cat?

Purr-plexed!

☆

When is the most likely time that an elephant will walk into your house?

When the door is open!

☆

Where did the kittens go on their school field trip?

To the mew-seum!

☆

What did the owl say when his friends went away?

Now I'm owl alone!

☆

What do cats like on a hot day?

Mice cream cones!

☆

What do you call a lion with chicken pox?

A dotted lion!

☆

How is a cowardly dog like a faucet?
They both run!

☆

What did the mother dog say to her puppy?
"We're eating dinner soon. Don't fill up on homework!"

☆

What do you get when you cross a sheepdog and a rose?
A collie-flower!

☆

What do you call an animal who eats his mother's sister?
An aunt eater!

☆

What's the last thing that goes through a bug's mind when it hits a car windshield?
Its butt!

Why did the bear wear a tank top?
Because he had the right to bear arms!

How do you make a dog float?

A small dog, two scoops of ice
cream, and soda water!

☆

**What do you call a bear with no
teeth?**

A gummy bear!

☆

**What happened when the dog
went to the flea circus?**

He stole the show!

☆

How do rabbits travel?

By hare plane!

☆

What do you call a bird that is afraid to fly?

Chicken!

☆

What do you call it when skunks argue?

Raising a stink!

☆

What's a wolf's favorite holiday?

Howl-o-ween!

☆

What looks like half a cat?

The other half!

☆

Why did the lion wear a hat?

He wanted to be a dandy-lion!

☆

**What do you call a camel without
   a hump?**

Hump-frey!

☆

**If you've seen one line catch an
   elephant, you've seen 'em
   maul!**

☆

**Why do sharks swim in salt
   water?**

Because pepper makes them sneeze!

☆

Why did the elephant leave the circus?

He was tired of working for peanuts!

☆

How do you catch a squirrel?

Climb a tree and act like a nut!

☆

What song do lions sing at Christmas?

Jungle Bells!

☆

Why isn't a dog a good boss?

Because they hound their employees!

☆

What is green and pecks on trees?

A Woodpickle!

☆

What state has the most cats and
dogs?

Petsylvania!

☆

What's worse than a giraffe with a
sore throat?

A centipede with athlete's foot!

☆

How do you know lions are
religious?

Because they prey often and as a
family!

☆

How do you know if there is a

gorilla in your refrigerator?

The door won't shut!

What's a cat's favorite dessert?

Chocolate mouse!

☆

THE LAUGH GIRAFFE'S
BEST AND FUNNIEST ANIMAL JOKES

What did the dog say as he left for work?

I'm going to the paw-ffice!

☆

Why don't penguins fly?

Because they're not tall enough to be pilots!

☆

Why did the snowman call his dog "Frost"?

Because he bites!

☆

Why did the cat go to the vet?

Because he wasn't feline well!

☆

**What do you call chickens
crossing the road?**

Poultry in motion!

☆

What subject are snakes good at?

Hiss-Tory!

☆

**How do you catch a unique
rabbit?**

Unique up on him!

☆

What do cats eat for breakfast?

Mice-crispies!

☆

What's the difference between an elephant and a banana?
You wouldn't want to peel an elephant!

☆

What did the elephant say when the man grabbed him by the tail?
That's the end of me!

☆

What is a cat's favorite song?
Three Blind Mice!

☆

What do you call lending money to a bison?

A buffa-loan!

☆

What kind of dog opens locks?

A corg-key!

☆

What animal do you find at a baseball game?

A bat!

☆

When does a duck wake up?

At the quack of dawn!

☆

What do you get when you cross a frog and a dog?

A croaker-spaniel.

☆

Why did the cat go to medical school?

To become a first aid kit!

☆

What's the difference between a tiger and a lion?

The tiger has the mane part missing!

☆

How does a cat sing the scales?

Do-re-mew!

☆

How do you make an octopus laugh?

With ten-tickles!

☆

What's a rabbit's favorite dance style?

Hip-Hop!

☆

What do you call a group of

rabbits hopping backwards?

A receding hare line!

☆

Why was the bear spoiled?

His mother panda'd to his every need!

☆

How do you get a hippo to tell the

truth?

You hippo-notize him!

What do a car, a tree, and an elephant have in common?

They all have trunks!

☆

What's invisible and smells like carrots?

Rabbit farts!

☆

What kind of dog is like a telephone?

One with collar-ID!

☆

What's gray and goes around and around?

An elephant in a washing machine!

☆

Where do fish sleep?

On the sea bed!

☆

Why did the bear leave the restaurant?

He thought the food was unbearable!

☆

Why did the pig leave the party?

Because everyone thought he was a boar!

☆

What do you call a dinosaur in a car accident?

A tyrannosaurus wreck!

☆

Why do mother kangaroos hate rainy days?

Because their kids have to play inside!

What do you get when you cross

an elephant and a fish?

Swimming trunks!

☆

What kind of fish is famous?

A starfish!

☆

Why did the sea lion laugh?

Because the joke was really seal-y!

☆

What animal is a good carpenter?

A hammerhead shark!

☆

What do you call a cow in an earthquake?

A milkshake!

☆

What do do you get if you cross a centipede with a parrot?

A walkie-talkie!

☆

What's the difference between a business man and an overheated dog?

The business man wears a suit. The dog just pants!

☆

What do you get if you cross a dog and a calculator?

A best friend you can really count on!

☆

What did the train conductor say to the kangaroo?

Hop on!

☆

Why is the barn so noisy?

Because the cows have horns!

☆

What is a polygon?

A dead parrot!

☆

What do you call a long-haired hippo?

A hippy!

☆

What do you call a sleeping dinosaur?

A dino-snore!

☆

What do you call a cat that eats lemons?

A sour puss!

☆

How many elephants can you put in an empty stadium?

One. After that it's not empty!

☆

What does a lion call a meerkat?

Fast food!

☆

How do Mexican sheep say Merry Christmas?

Fleece Navidad!

☆

What do you get when you cross a giraffe and a German shepherd?

A watchdog for thc cighth floor!

☆

How do you catch a rabbit?

Make a noise like a carrot!

☆

Have you ever seen a catfish?
No—how did he hold the rod and
   reel?

☆

**When is it bad luck to see a black
   cat?**
When you're a mouse!

☆

What do you call a cow band?
Moo-sicians!

☆

**Today I learned that a giraffe's
   neck is so strong you can climb
   up it.**
I also got banned from the zoo!

☆

Who's a penguin's favorite relative?

Aunt Arctica!

☆

I was going to tell you a cow joke,

But it's pasture bedtime!

☆

Where do famous dragons go when they retire?

The hall of flame!

☆

Why did the elephant paint his toenails red?

To hide in cherry trees!

☆

How many skunks does it take to make a big stink?

A phew!

☆

Why are apes good fighters?

They use gorilla warfare!

☆

What kind of sandals do frogs wear?

Open-toad!

☆

In what event did the kangaroo win a gold medal?

The long jump!

☆

What is a lion's favorite state?

Maine!

☆

**What do dolphins have that no
other animal has?**

Baby dolphins!

☆

What do you call a pig thief?

A ham-burglar!

☆

What do you a duck telling jokes?

A wise quacker!

☆

Why was the chicken sick?

He had people-pox!

☆

What kind of videos do ducks watch?

Duck-umentaries!

☆

What do you call an angry rabbit that got burned?

A hot cross bunnie!

☆

Where do penguins keep their money?

In a snow bank!

☆

Why did the man think he was a pony?

Because he was a little hoarse!

☆

What's a dog's favorite instrument?

A trom-bone!

☆

Why do ducks have webbed feet?

To stomp out forest fires!

☆

Why do elephants have flat feet?

To stomp out burning ducks!

☆

What game do elephants play with humans?

Squash!

☆

What do you give a sick bird?

Tweetment!

☆

What happened when the pig pen broke?

They had to use a pencil!

☆

Why do cows wear bells?

Because their horns are silent!

☆

What steps do you take if a rhinoceros is charging at you?

Big ones!

☆

How do birds learn to fly?

They just wing it!

☆

How do fish watch their weight?

With their scales!

☆

**What kind of monkey works in a
call center?**

A who-rang-utang!

What do you call a cow that

doesn't give milk?

An udder failure!

☆

What do you call a funny chicken?

A comedi-hen!

☆

What kind of dog chases anything

red?

A bull-dog!

☆

Why can't you see an elephant

hiding in a tree?

Because he's really good at it!

☆

What bird is always sad?

The blue jay!

☆

How do you spell mousetrap with only three letters?

C-A-T!

☆

When does a horse talk?

Whinny wants to!

☆

What did one fish say to the other?

Keep your mouth shut and you won't get caught!

☆

How do you stop an elephant from charging?

Take away his credit card!

☆

What has four legs, two trunks, and sunglasses?

An elephant on vacation!

☆

What is smarter than a talking cat?

A spelling bee!

☆

What do you call a ham you really want to eat?

Pork-u-pine!

☆

The early bird might get the worm . . .

But the second mouse gets the cheese!

☆

Why did the horse sneeze?

Hay fever!

☆

What does a clam do on its birthday?

Shell-ebrate!

☆

Why are frogs happy?

Because they eat what bugs them!

☆

How long are a horse's legs?

Long enough to reach the ground!

☆

What did one flea say to the other?

Should we walk or take a dog?

☆

How do fleas travel?

By itch-hiking!

☆

Why did the bee go to the doctor?

Because of his hives!

☆

THE LAUGH GIRAFFE'S
BEST AND FUNNIEST ANIMAL JOKES

What is black and white and red all over?

A sunburned penguin!

☆

How are elephants and trees alike?

They both have trunks!

☆

Why did the dog walk into the saloon?

He was looking for the man who shot his paw!

☆

What kind of monkey explodes?

A ba-boom!

☆

What do you get if you cross

fireworks and a duck?

A fire-quacker!

☆

What kind of snakes are found on

cars?

Windshield vipers!

☆

Why did the T-Rex eat raw meat?

Because its short arms couldn't

work the oven!

☆

Why can't you tell a pig a secret?

Because they always squeal!

☆

How do you stop a dog from digging in your garden?

Take away his shovel!

☆

What did the duck say when she bought lipstick?

Put it on my bill!

☆

What did the horse say when he fell?

I've fallen and I can't giddy up!

☆

Why aren't giraffes good pets?

They're very high maintenance!

☆

Why do stupid dogs have flat faces?

From chasing parked cars!

☆

Which side of a bear has the most fur?

The outside!

☆

What do you call a deer with no eyes?

No eye-deer!

☆

What do you say to a dog when you give him a treat?

Bone appetite!

☆

What are caterpillars afraid of?

Dogapillars!

☆

Why did the bird go to the library?

To find bookworms!

☆

How do spiders communicate?

Through the World Wide Web!

☆

What do you call a 400-pound gorilla?

Sir!

☆

What kind of duck steals things?

A robber duck!

☆

What do you get when you cross a pig and a tortoise?

A slow-pork!

☆

When does a platypus go "moo?"

When it's learning a new language!

☆

What's a cat's best subject in school?

Mew-sic!

☆

Why can't you hear a pterodactyl go to the bathroom?

Because the pee is silent!

☆

What do you call a man attacked by a cat?

Claude!

☆

What do frogs like to drink?

Croak-a-Cola!

☆

What is black and white and red all over?

A skunk with a rash!

☆

How does a dog stop a video?

With the paws button!

☆

One of the seven dwarfs kissed a giraffe . . .

The other six put him up to it!

☆

Did you hear about the sad horse?

He told a tale of "whoa!"

☆

THE LAUGH GIRAFFE'S
BEST AND FUNNIEST ANIMAL JOKES

Why didn't the Teddy Bear have dessert?

He was already stuffed!

☆

What kind of dog is the quietest?

A hush puppy!

☆

What do you do with a blue elephant?

Try to cheer him up!

☆

When isn't chicken soup good for your health?

When you're the chicken!

☆

How do you know that bears don't wear shoes?

Because they go around bear-footed!

☆

Why are cats bad story tellers?

Because they only have one tale!

☆

What do you call a polar bear in the jungle?

Lost!

☆

What did the dog say when he sat on sandpaper?

Rufff!

☆

Why did the man bring a cow to his house?

He needed a lawn-mooer!

☆

Why do cows have hoofs instead of feet?

Because they lactose!

☆

What do you get from a pampered cow?

Spoiled milk!

☆

What kind of cows live at the North Pole?

Eski-moos!

☆

What has four legs and goes oom-oom?

A cow walking backwards!

☆

What do you call a cow with only two legs?

Lean beef!

☆

What do you call a cow with no legs?

Ground beef!

☆

What do you call a pig with no legs?

A ground hog!

☆

Can a kangaroo jump higher than the Empire State Building?

Of course! Buildings can't jump!

☆

What do you call a pig that knows karate?

Pork chop!

☆

What is the elephant's favorite vegetable?

Squash!

☆

Where do baby apes sleep?

In ape-ri-cots!

☆

What do you call a zoo with just giraffes?

Giraffic Park!

☆

What's black and white, black and white, black and white, and green?

Three skunks fighting over a pickle!

☆

THE LAUGH GIRAFFE'S
BEST AND FUNNIEST ANIMAL JOKES

What do caterpillars study in school?

Mothamatics!

☆

It takes a big man to admit his mistakes . . .

It takes an even bigger man to give a giraffe a haircut!

☆

What's black and white and noisy?

A zebra playing drums!

☆

Who makes dinosaur clothes?

A Dino-sewer!

☆

Where do you find a dog with no legs?

Exactly where you left him!

☆

Why does a flamingo raise one leg when it stands?

Because if it raised two legs it would fall down!

☆

What did the cowboy say when his dog ran away?

Well, doggone!

☆

How did the tree scare the cat?

With its bark!

☆

What do you call a dog with no legs?

Doesn't make any difference. He won't come to you!

☆

Where does a cow go to see art?

The moo-seum!

☆

What kind of cats like bowling?

Alley cats!

☆

Where does the elephant keep his luggage?

In his trunk!

☆

What kind of deer is worth a dollar?

A buck!

☆

What's big and gray, sings and wears a mask?

The elephantom of the opera!

☆

What kind of dog loves a bath?

A sham-poodle!

☆

How do camels hide?

With camel-flage!

☆

How does a cow sneak off a farm?

Right pasteurize!

☆

Why do gorillas have large nostrils?

Because they have fat fingers!

☆

Why aren't leopards good at playing hide and seek?

Because they are always spotted!

☆

Why did the dog cross the road twice?

He was trying to fetch a boomerang!

☆

What do you call the king of the giraffes?

Your Royal Highness!

Where is the best place for a barking dog?

A barking lot!

☆

What do you give a pig with a rash?

Oink-ment!

☆

What is big and blue?

An elephant holding his breath!

☆

Why wasn't the giraffe invited to the party?

He was a big pain in the neck!

☆

Why didn't the skunk smell?

Because he had a cold!

☆

What do cows use in texts?

E-moo-jis!

☆

What goes tick-tock, bow-wow?

A watch dog!

☆

What do you call twin ocptopuses?

I-tenticle!

☆

What do you get when you cross a giraffe and an ant?

A gi-ant!

☆

Why are elephants wrinkled?

Because they don't fit on an ironing
  board!

☆

**What happens when a frog's car
  breaks down?**

It gets toad away!

☆

**Why did the lion throw up after
  he ate the priest?**

It's hard to keep a good man down!

☆

**What animals have more lives
  than cats?**

Frogs. They croak all the time!

☆

Why did the giraffe get promoted in his job?

Because people looked up to him!

☆

How do you know an elephant has been on your refrigerator?

Footprints in the butter!

☆

What is a giraffe's favorite fruit?

Neck-tarines!

☆

How do bees go to school?

On the school buzz!

☆

What would you do if an elephant sat in front of you at the movies?

Miss most of the movie!

☆

What do you do if a cat swallows your pencil?

Use a pen!

☆

What is as big as an elephant but weighs nothing?

Its shadow!

☆

What two dinosaurs go to the rodeo?

The bronco-saurus and the tyrannosaurus Tex!

☆

What do you call a giraffe that swallowed a toy jet?

A plane in the neck!

☆

What do you call a shark with a tie?

So-fishticated!

☆

Why was the pig a bad driver?

Because he was a road hog!

☆

What do you call a chicken that wakes you up?

An alarm cluck!

☆

What does a calf become after it is one year old?

Two years old!

☆

What sound do porcupines make when they kiss?

Ouch!

☆

Why did the policeman give the sheep a ticket?

He made an illegal ewe turn!

☆

What do you get if you cross and elephant and a sparrow?

Broken telephone lines!

☆

What do you give a dog with a fever?

Mustard! It's the best thing for a hot dog!

☆

What kind of dinosaur never gives up?

A try and try and try-ceratops!

☆

What do you use to count cows?

A cow-culator!

☆

What do you call a twitching cow?

Beef jerky!

☆

What do you call a wild dog that meditates?

Aware-wolf!

☆

What does a cat say when his tail is stepped on?

Me-owwww!

☆

Have you heard the joke about the giraffe's neck?

It's a long one!

☆

Why didn't people laugh at the giraffe joke?

Because it went over their heads!

☆

What did the duck do after he read all these jokes?

He quacked up!

☆

Do You Have More Animal Jokes You Love? Add Them Here and Tell All Your Friends!

_____

_____

_____

_____

_____

_____

_____

_____

_____

_____

_____

_____

_____

_____

_____

_____